Understanding Mental Illness

Written by Susan Foley, MD
and Regen Foley

Production Date: September 2018

Plant & Location: Printed in Paju-Si, South Korea by Artin Printing Co.

Job/Batch: #82203

Layout, Illustrations, and Cover Design by Regen Foley

Requests for permission to make copies of any part of this work should be mailed to:
The Sunshine Project, Inc
1004 Grand Isle Way
Palm Beach Gardens, FL 33418 Or via our website: www.sunshineproj.org

ISBN: 978-1719128384

A special thanks to:

The Sunshine Project, Inc.

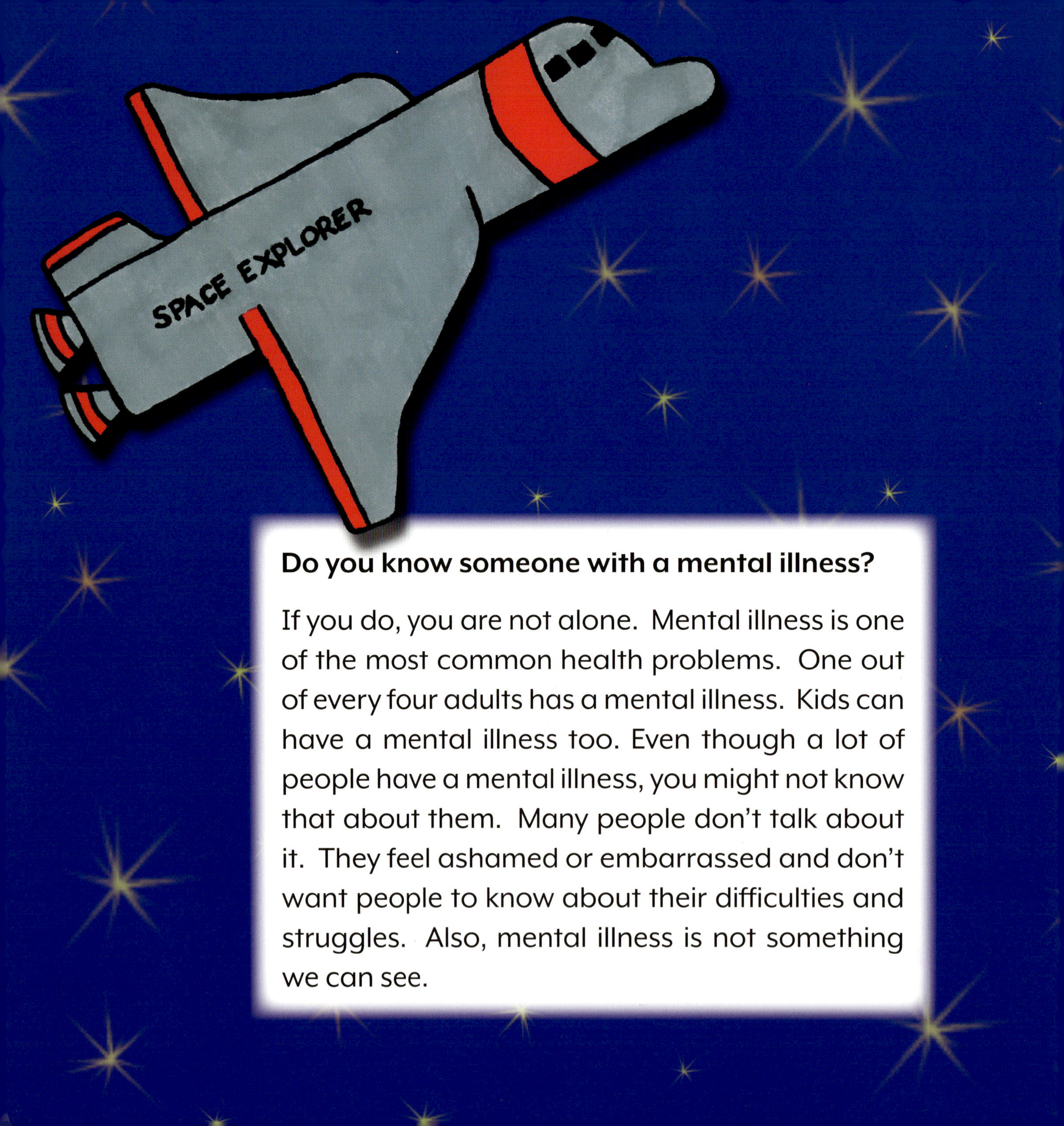

Do you know someone with a mental illness?

If you do, you are not alone. Mental illness is one of the most common health problems. One out of every four adults has a mental illness. Kids can have a mental illness too. Even though a lot of people have a mental illness, you might not know that about them. Many people don't talk about it. They feel ashamed or embarrassed and don't want people to know about their difficulties and struggles. Also, mental illness is not something we can see.

Hopefully things are changing so people won't feel this way. When people feel like they can talk about mental illness, it will help everyone: the mentally ill people, their families, and their community, including all of us who are impacted by mental illness. When sick people don't feel ashamed about their illness, they are more likely to get help. More people can get the help they need when all of us are more aware of how large this problem is.

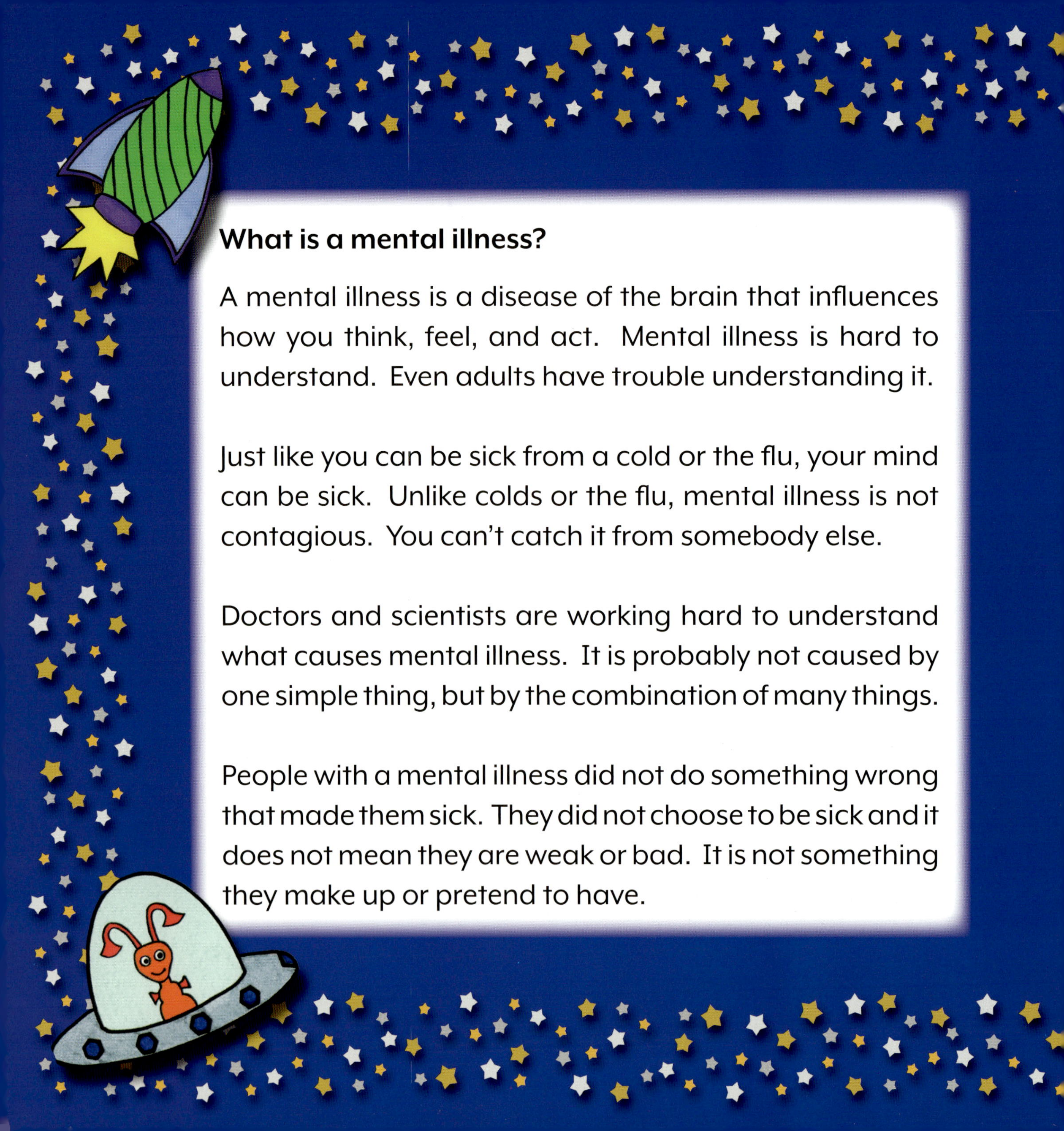

What is a mental illness?

A mental illness is a disease of the brain that influences how you think, feel, and act. Mental illness is hard to understand. Even adults have trouble understanding it.

Just like you can be sick from a cold or the flu, your mind can be sick. Unlike colds or the flu, mental illness is not contagious. You can't catch it from somebody else.

Doctors and scientists are working hard to understand what causes mental illness. It is probably not caused by one simple thing, but by the combination of many things.

People with a mental illness did not do something wrong that made them sick. They did not choose to be sick and it does not mean they are weak or bad. It is not something they make up or pretend to have.

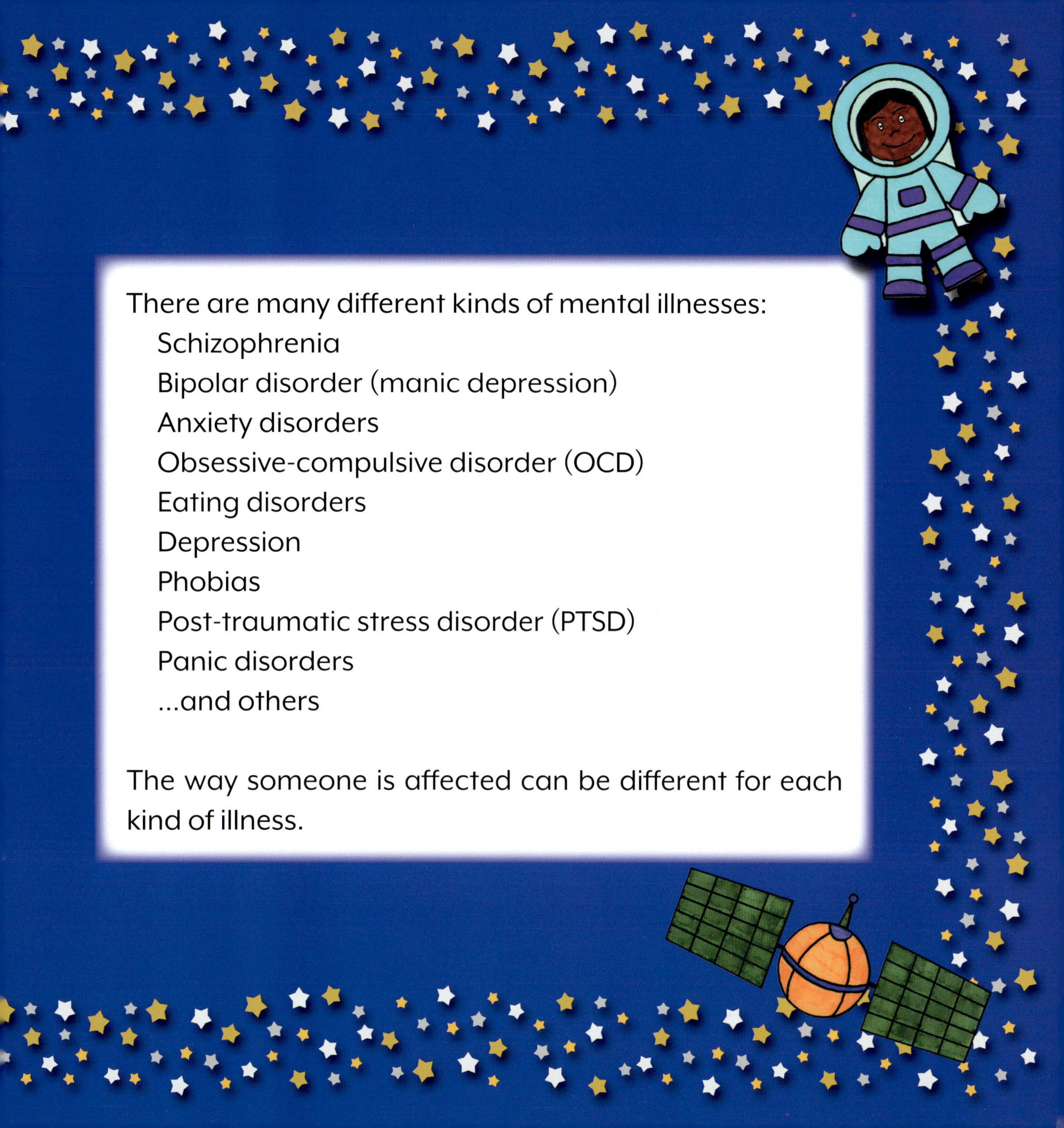

There are many different kinds of mental illnesses:

- Schizophrenia
- Bipolar disorder (manic depression)
- Anxiety disorders
- Obsessive-compulsive disorder (OCD)
- Eating disorders
- Depression
- Phobias
- Post-traumatic stress disorder (PTSD)
- Panic disorders
- ...and others

The way someone is affected can be different for each kind of illness.

How does mental illness affect people?

Each person with a mental illness will have different experiences. Even people with the same illness may feel or act differently. It can be mild in some people and severe in others.

A person can be affected by their illness in different ways at different times. They may get worse, stay the same, or get better. Sometimes it comes and goes over a long time. Some people struggle with mental illness all their lives. They need treatment forever. Other people have one or more episodes and they are fine in between. Some people get better and never need treatment again.

Mental illness can make a person act very differently from the way they normally act. Many of the ways the person feels or acts are normal emotions or behaviors that everyone experiences. In the sick person they are larger than usual or last a lot longer than you would expect. Sometimes people with a mental illness can act in strange, confusing, or even scary ways.

The illness may cause the person to:

- Cry
- Feel sad all the time
- Sleep all the time or not sleep at all
- Drink too much alcohol or take drugs
- Have trouble getting out of bed
- Talk to themselves
- Say things that don't make sense
- Have trouble eating or eat too much
- Have trouble talking to people
- Not think clearly
- Have trouble getting along with others
- Struggle to do regular activities

They might also act:

Grouchy
Angry
Hyper (overactive)
Impatient
Confused

Sometimes they might do things that scare you like:

Loose their temper
Yell
Act mean
Break things
Hurt themselves or others
Act like they can't see, hear, or feel anything

Mental illness can even affect the way a person looks. Sometimes they don't shower or change their clothes or comb their hair. The expressions on the person's face might even change for no reason.

How can people with a mental illness get better?

It is the job of the doctors, counselors, and other adults to help the sick person. There are special medicines for different kinds of mental illnesses. There are also different kinds of therapies. One kind of therapy is talking to a trained doctor or counselor. Other kinds involve music, art, dance, and exercise. These are activities that make all of us feel better. It can take weeks or even months of treatment for them to get better, so don't be worried if the treatments don't make them better right away.

Doctors and scientists are looking for better ways to treat mental illnesses. New treatments are discovered all the time.

Sometimes when a person with a mental illness is very sick they are taken by the police or emergency crews to the hospital against their will. This can be very frightening for them and for their family and friends. If this happens, remember that your loved one does not understand that they need help and they are being taken to a place where they will be safe and can get better.

The person you love may also choose to go to a hospital or special clinic and stay for a long time so that they can get help. Once they feel better, they will come home. This could take days, weeks, or sometimes even months, but they will not be gone forever.

Remember:

There is a lot of hope. There are all kinds of treatments available to help.

People with mental illness can live happy productive lives when they get the help they need.

How are the family and loved ones of a person with a mental illness impacted?

It is hard to have someone in your life with a mental illness. A sick family member affects the whole family.

Mental illness can make life with your family very different. Sometimes it seems like the sick person takes over your normal family life and you may feel like that's not fair. You may also miss the fun times you used to have.

You are probably very worried for your loved one. You might also be worried about your family, and about yourself.

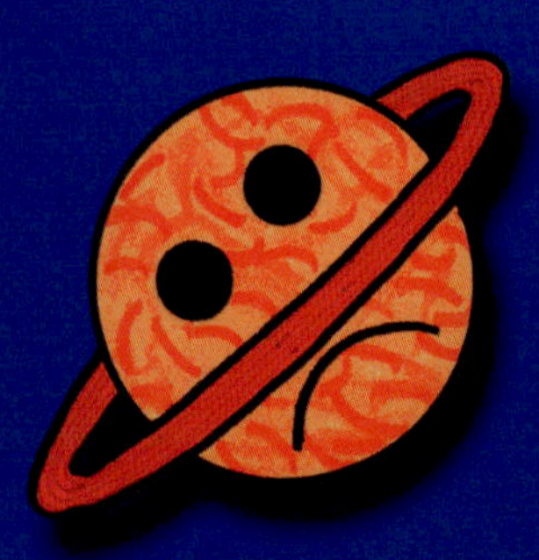

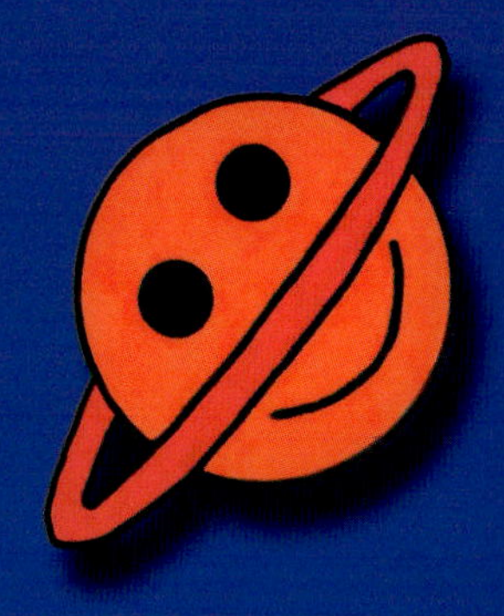

You might feel:

- Sad
- Angry
- Confused
- Scared
- Lonely
- Relieved (when they are doing better or when they go to the hospital)
- Embarrassed
- Tense
- Worried
- Frightened

It is ok to have these feelings. Lots of people do! Even adults. Your feelings can change from day to day or even throughout a day.

What can you do to feel better?

It is not your fault this person is sick. You did not do anything to make this happen. There is nothing you can do to make them better. That is the job of trained adults.

You CAN do things to make yourself feel better:

Do things you enjoy at home: read, do art projects, play with friends.

Do fun activities outside your home such as play sports, visit a friend, or join a club.

It is OK to have happy times even when things are not happy for your loved one.

Be supportive of your sick loved one and other family members.
Get support from friends and caring adults.
Participate in activities that help others like a volunteer project.

When you feel sad, confused, or have questions, find an adult you trust to talk to. It could be a family member, a teacher, a counselor, a coach, a doctor, or a religious leader. If you are worried about your safety or the safety of your family, say something right away. It is OK to reach out for help. It is important for you to talk about your feelings.

Some of your questions for your trusted adult might be:

Will my loved one get better?

Will my loved one be ok?

Why did this happen to us?

Is this my fault?

Who will take care of me while my loved one is sick?

Who will take care of my sick loved one?

Mental illness can make people say mean things. It is not the way they really feel. If they were healthy they would not say these things to you. They still love you. That can be hard to remember while it is happening. Maybe you can think of a time you were really tired or sick, and you said something that you did not really mean.

A lot of people don't understand mental illness. They might make fun of it and that can hurt your feelings. You may want to think about things to say if anyone says something mean or stupid about the sick person you love. You may want to practice what you want to say.

- "My loved one can't help the way they act because they are sick."
- "My loved one is getting help from the doctor just like everybody gets help from the doctor when they are sick."
- "I know you are making fun of my loved one because you are scared. There is no need to be scared. They won't hurt you."
- "My loved one is working on getting better."
- "Even though my loved one is sick, I love them very much."
- You can also choose not to say anything at all and ignore the questions or mean comments.

Having to deal with difficult times is not fun,
but it can help you become a stronger person.
It can even make you a better person.

Remember:
You are not responsible!
Nothing you did made your loved one sick.
You can't make them better. That's the job of trained adults.
The person acts this way because they are sick.
It is OK to ask for help.
With help your loved one can get better.

ABOUT THE AUTHORS

Susan E. Foley, M.D., F.A.A.P. is a board certified pediatrician who lives and works in South Florida. Involved in many non-profit organizations that serve the welfare and mental health of children and families, she served on the board of several of these organizations. Her husband died of cancer in 1998. She found few resources available to help her daughter at this difficult time, so together they wrote their first book, <u>Close to My Heart</u>, to help other children faced with the death of a loved one. The success of that book inspired them to write other books for children facing difficult issues.

Regen Foley is a graduate of Tulane University and Georgetown University School of Foreign Service. She has been involved in community service all of her life. Regen lost her beloved stepfather to cancer on her tenth birthday. In his honor she founded and runs her own non- profit organization, The Sunshine Project, Inc. [a 501(c)(3)]. She survived a life threatening illness herself at the age of fifteen. Her life experiences and her compassion for others are her inspiration for her books.